23258

23258

First Facts™

Learning about Money

Goods and Services

by Janeen R. Adil

Consultant:
Sharon M. Danes, PhD
Professor and Family Economist
University of Minnesota

Capstone press

Mankato, Minnesota

First Facts is published by Capstone Press,
151 Good Counsel Drive, P.O. Box 669, Mankato, Minnesota 56002.
www.capstonepress.com

Library of Congress Cataloging-in-Publication Data
Adil, Janeen R.
    Goods and services / by Janeen R. Adil.
    p. cm. — (First facts. Learning about money)
    Summary: "Simple text and photographs explain what goods and services are and their
role in earning income and spending money. Includes an activity and fun facts"—Provided by
publisher.
    Includes bibliographical references and index.
    ISBN-13: 978-0-7368-5395-8 (hardcover)
    ISBN-10: 0-7368-5395-2 (hardcover)
    1. Commerce—Juvenile literature. 2. Consumer goods—Juvenile literature. 3. Service
industries—Juvenile literature. 4. Purchasing—Juvenile literature. 5. Selling—Juvenile literature. I.
Title. II. Series.
HF5392.A38 2006
338.4—dc22   2005019574

Editorial Credits
Wendy Dieker, editor; Jennifer Bergstrom, set designer; Bobbi J. Dey, book designer;
    Jo Miller, photo researcher/photo editor

Photo Credits
Art Directors/Spencer Grant, 9; Capstone Press/Karon Dubke, cover, 6 (right), 14–15, 16–17, 19;
Corbis/Ariel Skelley, 5; Corbis Royalty Free, 7; David R. Frazier Photolibrary, 10; Digital Vision,
6 (left); Getty Images Inc./Yellow Dog Productions, 11; The Granger Collection, New York, 20;
Unicorn Stock Photos/D. Yeske, 12–13

1 2 3 4 5 6 11 10 09 08 07 06

Table of Contents

Things People Buy

People buy things they need and want. They buy **goods** and **services**. Goods are real things that people can touch and use. A service is work done for other people.

An eye doctor does a service as he checks your eyes. The glasses he sells are goods.

Fun Fact!
In 2004, the U.S. Department of Labor counted over 10 million people making goods in U.S. factories.

4

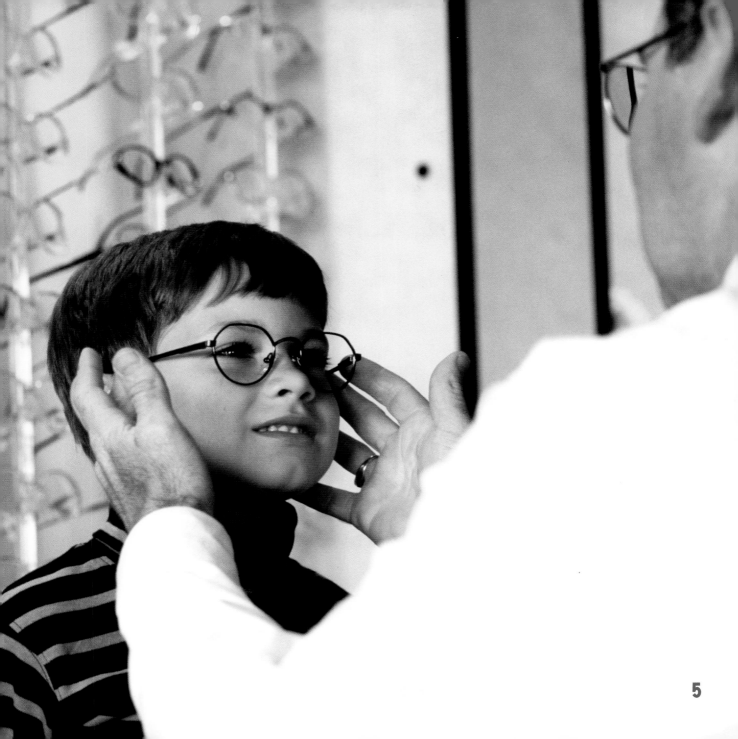

Goods and Services

Goods can be large, like a house or a car. Goods can also be small. Notebooks, a bunch of bananas, and soap are some small goods.

Men, women, boys, and girls can all do services. A dentist's work is a service. Washing cars, mowing lawns, and cutting hair are other services.

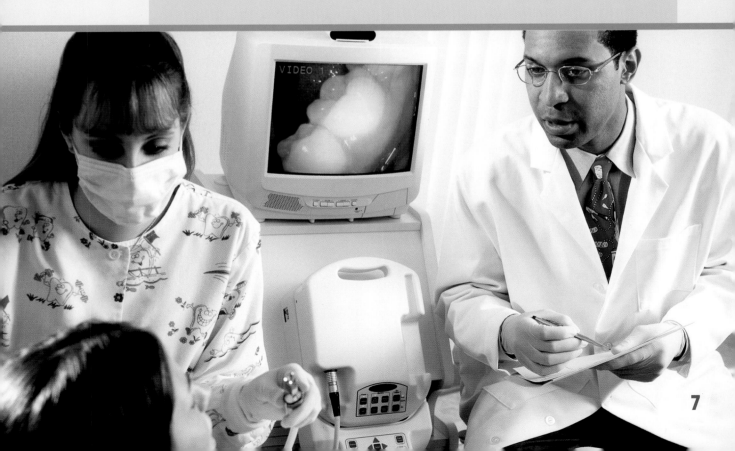

Government Services

Some goods and services come from the **government**. The government collects money called **taxes**. Taxes pay for the goods and services everyone uses. Taxes pay for firefighters and police officers. Parks, libraries, and schools are also paid for with taxes.

! Fun Fact!
In 1921, West Virginia became the first state to collect taxes on goods people bought in stores.

Producers

Goods and services are sold by **producers**. Farmers sell the vegetables they grow. Mechanics are producers when they sell the service of fixing cars.

Kids can also be producers. Tim sells a service when he delivers newspapers. He can also sell the cookies he baked.

Consumers

Anyone who buys and uses goods and services is a **consumer**. Consumers choose what goods and services they buy. Jenna is a consumer. She uses her money to buy a new bike.

Fun Fact!

U.S. teens spend over $160 billion of their own money each year.

Earning Income

Producers **earn** money, or **income**. As a producer, Mary sells candy in her shop to earn money. Then she uses her income to buy goods and services from others. Mary is a consumer when she buys meat from the market.

Baseball
Cards
2 for $1.00

16

Joe Is a Producer

Joe sells clothes and toys he doesn't use anymore. By selling these goods, Joe is a producer. He earns income that he can spend on other goods and services.

Joe Is a Consumer

As a consumer, Joe makes choices about his income. He saves part of his money for camp next summer. He buys some school supplies he needs. Then he has money left to buy a book he wants. What goods and services do you buy?

Taxes have been around for about 5,000 years. In ancient Egypt, people paid many taxes. The king collected them at least once a year. Ancient Egyptian art shows workers counting and recording the taxes.

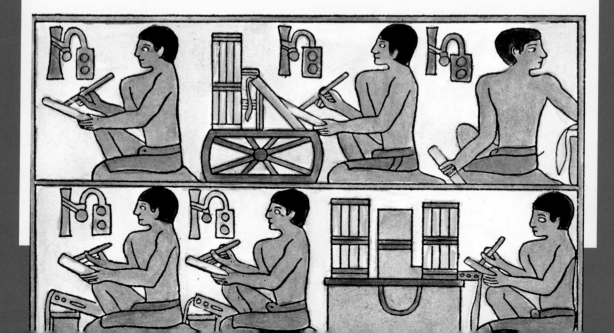

Hands On: In and Out

Every family sells goods and services to earn money. This money buys the goods and services a family needs and wants. Where does your family's income come from? Where does income go?

What You Need

paper
markers, crayons, or
   colored pencils

What You Do

1. Draw a picture of your home.
2. Draw arrows pointing to the home. Write the goods or services people in your family sell to make money on each arrow.
3. Draw arrows pointing away from the house. On each arrow, write where your family's income goes. Think of as many goods and services as you can. Families buy things like food and clothing. Does your family buy pet food, movie tickets, haircuts, or trips too?

Talk about your picture with your family. Did you forget any goods or services? How many things does your family want and need? You may be surprised!

Glossary

consumer (kuhn-SOO-mur)—a person who buys and uses goods and services

earn (URN)—to receive payment for working

goods (GUDZ)—real things that a person can touch and use

government (GUHV-urn-muhnt)—the people who lead a country, state, or city

income (IN-kuhm)—money a person receives for doing a job

producer (pruh-DOOSS-uhr)—a person who sells goods and services

service (SUR-viss)—work that's done for other people

taxes (TAKS-uhz)—money the government collects to use for providing goods and services

Read More

Firestone, Mary. *Earning Money.* Learning about Money. Mankato, Minn: Capstone Press, 2005.

Godfrey, Neale S. *Neale S. Godfrey's Ultimate Kids' Money Book.* New York: Simon & Schuster Books for Young Readers, 1998.

Ridgway, Tom. *The Young Zillionaire's Guide to Buying Goods and Services.* Be a Zillionaire. New York: Rosen, 2000.

Internet Sites

FactHound offers a safe, fun way to find Internet sites related to this book. All of the sites on FactHound have been researched by our staff.

Here's how:
1. Visit *www.facthound.com*
2. Type in this special code **0736853952** for age-appropriate sites. Or enter a search word related to this book for a more general search.
3. Click on the **Fetch It** button.

FactHound will fetch the best sites for you!

Index